EXPERIMENTS WITH PLANTS

A TRUE BOOK

by

Salvatore Tocci

Children's Press®
A Division of Scholastic Inc.

New York Toronto London Auckland Sydney
Mexico City New Delhi Hong Kong
Danbury, Connecticut

Seeds
sprouting

Reading Consultant
Nanci Vargus
*Primary Multiage Teacher
Decatur Township Schools,
Indianapolis, IN*

Science Consultant
Robert Lange
*Associate Professor
Brandeis University*

**The author and publisher are
not responsible for injuries or
accidents that occur during or
from any experiments.
Experiments should be conducted
in the presence of or with the
help of an adult. Any instructions
of the experiments that require
the use of sharp, hot, or other
unsafe items should be
conducted by or with the
help of an adult.**

Library of Congress Cataloging-in-Publication Data

Tocci, Salvatore.
    Experiments with plants / by Salvatore Tocci.
        p. cm.—(A true book)
    Includes bibliographical references and index (p.).
    ISBN 0-516-22252-X   (lib. bdg.) 0-516-27351-5   (pbk.)
    1. Botany—Experiments—Juvenile literature. 2. Plants—Experiments—
Juvenile literature. [1. Botany—Experiments—Juvenile literature. 2. Plants—
Experiments—Juvenile literature. 3. Experiments.] I. Title. II. Series.

QK52.6.T628 2001
580—dc21   00-052118

Contents

To stay alive, an African elephant must eat more than 500 pounds (227 kg) of food a day.

What Is the Largest Living Thing?

Can you name the largest living thing in the world? You may think it is an African elephant. An African elephant can be 13 feet (4 meters) tall and weigh 7 tons (6.3 metric tons). Despite its huge size, though, the African elephant is not the largest living thing in the world.

Maybe you think a blue whale is the largest living thing in the world. Although not as tall as an African elephant, a blue whale can reach a length of almost 120 feet (36.5 m) and can weigh 145 tons (131.5 metric tons). Even so, the blue whale is not the largest living thing in the world.

The largest living thing in the world is an aspen tree in Utah. This tree weighs about 6,600 tons (5,986 metric tons), or more than 45 times the weight

At birth, a blue whale (left) is over 20 feet (6.1 m) long and weighs about 2 tons (1.8 metric tons). This quaking aspen tree (right), called Pando, is located in the Wasatch Mountain Range of Utah. It spreads out to cover 200 acres (81 hectares), an area that equals about 140 football fields.

of a blue whale. The largest living thing in the world then is not an animal, but a plant.

What Is a Plant?

Plants can be found everywhere on Earth. Most plants live on land, but some live in oceans, rivers, lakes, and ponds. Plants can be found growing in a desert or living in snow and ice. Some plants can grow only where there is plenty of soil. Others grow

The plant floating in this pond is called duckweed. Duckweed helps the environment by naturally removing unclean things from the water where the plant lives.

where there are plenty of rocks and very little soil.

Plants come in all different sizes and shapes. Redwood trees, the tallest living things

A giant redwood, found in California, is the tallest living thing in the world.

in the world, grow over 300 feet (91.5 m), or as high as a 30-story building. Some plants are so small that you need a magnifying lens to study them. Some plants have tiny, pointed leaves. Other plants have big, broad leaves. Many plants produce beautiful, colorful flowers, while others don't have any flowers. Is there anything in common with all these different plants? All plants need certain things to live.

Drying Out

You will need:
- celery stalk
- knife
- ruler
- refrigerator
- sugar
- tablespoon
- small glass of water

Please ask an adult to help you cut a piece of celery stalk about 6 inches long. Place the stalk in the refrigerator and wait three days. Then remove the stalk from the refrigerator. Try to hold the stalk upright. What happens? Did the top bend?

This happens because the celery lost water while it was in the refrigerator.

Without water, plants begin to wilt and may die.

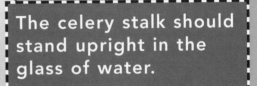

The celery stalk should stand upright in the glass of water.

Without water, the celery shrivels or wilts.

If the celery has not wilted too much, the stalk will bend a little. If this is the case, cut about a 1/2-inch from one end of the stalk. Then add 1 tablespoon of sugar to a small glass of water. Stir the water to dissolve the sugar. Stand the celery stalk in the glass of water. After two days, remove the stalk from the glass. Hold it upright. Does the top still bend? Chew on a piece of the stalk. How does it taste?

As the celery stood in the glass, the water and dissolved sugar moved up through the stalk. The water in the glass moved into the stalk by a process called osmosis. Because of osmosis, the celery stalk can stand upright again. Like all other living things, plants need water to live. Is there something, however, that only plants need to live?

Experiment 2

Soaking Up the Sun

You will need:
- grass seed
- shallow aluminum pan
- potting soil
- piece of cardboard

Plant some grass seed in an aluminum pan filled with potting soil. Water the soil and place the pan in a sunny spot. Keep the soil moist for about a week. Once the grass has grown about a 1/2-inch high, cover the grass at one end with a piece of cardboard. After a week, remove the cardboard. Compare the grass exposed to the sun with the grass that was covered by the cardboard.

Do not overwater the soil. Too much water will prevent the grass seed from growing.

The cardboard blocked the sunlight from reaching the grass. Without light, plants cannot grow. Plants need light and water to carry out a process called photosynthesis. Through photosynthesis, the plants create the nutrients, or food, they need to live. Unlike animals, plants are living things that can make their own food. Is there anything else besides water and light that plants need for photosynthesis?

Taking Out the Color

You will need:
- measuring cup
- small pot
- large green leaf
- stove
- fork
- water
- small glass
- rubbing alcohol

Add 1 cup of water to a small pot. Place the leaf in the water. Please ask an adult to help you boil the leaf for one minute. Allow the pot to cool. Remove the leaf with a fork and place it in a small glass filled with rubbing alcohol. Then set the glass in a pot of warm water for about an hour.

Be sure that the water in the pot is warm and not hot.

RUBBING ALCOHOL

Notice that the rubbing alcohol turned green. Use a fork to remove the leaf. Notice that the leaf has lost its green color. Leaves are green because they contain a chemical called chlorophyll. Warm rubbing alcohol takes out the chlorophyll from a leaf. In addition to water and light, plants also need chlorophyll for photo-synthesis.

Photosynthesis makes the nutrients plants need to live. Photosynthesis also makes the oxygen that all plants and animals need to survive.

Besides water, light, and chlorophyll, plants need one more thing for photosynthesis. This is a gas called carbon dioxide. Once they have all these things, plants make their own nutrients to live and grow.

How Do Plants Grow?

Like most plants, the giant aspen tree in Utah grew from a tiny seed. Seeds can be found everywhere, including your kitchen. We eat many types of seeds, including sunflower seeds, sesame seeds, corn, peas, beans, and peanuts. We

Bread is made with flour.
Flour is made from grinding
up the seeds of wheat plants.

also eat foods that are made
from seeds.

Like the plants that they
grow into, seeds come in all

A coconut is a very large seed. Inside the seed is the coconut meat that many people like to eat.

sizes and shapes. Most are very small, but some are quite large. No matter how tiny or large, all seeds can be thought of as packages with things inside. What's inside these packages?

Experiment 4

Examining Seeds

You will need:
- magnifying glass
- lima beans
- small jar
- food coloring
- teaspoon

Using the magnifying glass, examine one lima bean. The bean is a seed. Use your fingernail to try to remove the outer coating that covers the bean. This outer coating protects the seed and helps keep it moist.

The coating that surrounds a seed is difficult to remove.

Fill the jar halfway with water. Add about 25 drops of food coloring and stir. Soak several other lima beans in the colored water for two days. The water will soften the outer coating. The food coloring will make the parts inside the seeds easier to see. Remove the coating with your fingernail. Then use your fingernail to break the seed into two halves.

Examine the inside of a split seed with the magnifying glass. Do you see the embryo and food that are inside the seed? The lower part of the embryo will grow into a root. The upper part will grow to make a stem and leaves. The rest of the seed is the food. It will nourish the growing plant until it can make its own food through photosynthesis.

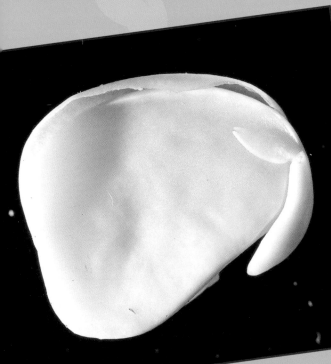

The embryo inside a seed is the baby plant. Notice that the food takes up more space than the embryo.

All seeds contain food. This food supplies the materials and energy needed for a seed to grow into a plant. For this to happen, a seed also needs the right conditions. The air must not be too hot or too cold, and it must be filled with oxygen. Also, the seed needs water. Once the seed gets all these things, it grows, or germinates. As the seed germinates, the stem and root will grow. Which way will the stem grow? Which way will the root grow?

Experiment 5

Germinating Seeds

You will need:
- large jar
- paper towels
- bean seeds

Fill the jar with damp paper towels. Place several bean seeds along the inside of the jar so that they can be seen through the glass. Be sure to keep the paper towels damp, but do not overwater them. Wait several days until the seeds begin to germinate. In which direction are the roots growing?

Place enough damp towels in the jar so they hold the bean seeds against the jar.

Next, turn the jar upside down so that the roots are heading upward. The towels should hold the seeds in place against the jar. Allow the roots to continue growing for several more days. Be sure to keep the towels moist. Notice that the roots turn around and again begin to grow downward.

Clean out the jar. Again, fill it with damp paper towels and place several bean seeds inside. Keep the jar near a window. This time, wait until the seeds germinate to make stems that grow upward. Place the jar on its side. Watch the stems as they continue to grow. The stems should turn and grow upward.

Stems will twist and turn so that they always grow upward.

Plants that grow close to one another have to compete for water, light, and everything else they need to live.

Some plants such as sunflowers naturally spread their own seeds along the ground.

Wherever the seeds fall, they begin to germinate. When this happens, the plants will be found growing close to one another. There are times when this can be a problem. For example, if there isn't a lot of water, some of the plants may not survive.

Seeds of other plants can be spread out in several different ways. Many types of seeds are spread by animals. Some seeds have hooks that

The tiny hooks provide these seeds with a "free ride" by sticking to an animal's fur.

get caught on an animal's fur. As the animal moves about, the seeds become loose and drop to the ground.

Experiment 6

💡

Scattering Seeds

Collect as many different types of seeds as you can. You may pick out the seeds from fruits or you may buy seeds used for growing flowers. Keep a record of the types of seeds you use.

Spread out the bed sheet in a garage or outdoors

You can find a variety of fruit or flower seeds at a nursery or hardware store.

on a flat surface. Plug in the fan and turn it on to its lowest speed. Hold the seeds in your hand at least 6 inches away from the fan. The breeze from the fan will scatter the seeds, just like the wind. Which seeds travel the shortest distance? The greatest distance? Use the measuring tape to find out how far these seeds traveled.

Please keep your hands away from the fan when you are holding out the seeds.

What Are the Parts of a Plant?

A plant that grows from a seed has three basic parts. These parts are the root, stem, and leaves. Roots secure the plant in the ground and absorb water and other nutrients to help it grow. How much water can a root absorb?

Experiment 7

Absorbing Water

You will need:
- measuring cup
- large jar with wide opening
- plastic wrap
- small potted plant
- small paint brush
- small knife
- water

Using a measuring cup, pour water into the jar so that it is nearly full. Write down how much water you poured into the jar. Cover the jar with plastic wrap.

Carefully remove the plant from the pot. Try not to damage the roots. Use the brush to remove as much soil as possible from the roots. Please ask an adult to help you cut a slit in the plastic wrap that covers the jar. Gently push the roots through the slit so that they fall into the water. Then adjust the plant so that it rests on top of the plastic wrap. If the slit opens wider, cover the opening with more plastic wrap.

Cover the opening with the plastic wrap so the water cannot evaporate.

Wait twenty-four hours. Remove the plastic wrap and plant from the jar. Use the measuring cup to find out how much water is left in the jar. Subtract this amount of water from the amount of water you first poured into the jar. That number is the amount of water the roots absorbed. Try the experiment again with different plants to find out if those roots absorb different amounts of water over twenty-four hours. Try to use plants that are about the same size and have about the same amount of roots.

Most plants have broad, flat leaves, such as oak, maple, and sycamore leaves. Did you know that evergreen needles and cactus spines are leaves, too?

The stems of a plant keep it up or support it. Stems also help to get water from the roots to the leaves. Water is used by the leaves for photosynthesis. Do leaves do anything else besides carry out photosynthesis?

Losing Water

You will need:
- houseplant with broad flat leaves
- plastic bag
- twist tie

Tie a plastic bag over several leaves of a household plant, such as a geranium. Place the plant in direct sunlight for several hours. Look closely inside the bag. What do you see? The water that collects inside the bag evaporated out of the leaves.

Can you find the
tiny openings
shown in this leaf?

Leaves have tiny
openings that allow
water to evaporate.
About 90 percent of
the water taken in
by the roots evapo-
rates through the
leaves. Most of the
water the plant
keeps is used for
photosynthesis.

The bright colors of flowers attract insects and birds, which carry pollen from one flower to another. Pollen are tiny, usually yellow grains that fertilize a flower to produce seeds.

In addition to roots, stems, and leaves, many plants also have flowers. A flower is the part that a plant uses to make new plants. Flowers make the seeds that germinate into new plants.

Fun With Plants

Now that you've learned about plants, here's a fun experiment to do.

Most people like flowers with striking colors, like red, yellow, and purple. Learn how you can turn a flower that has no color into one that has more than one color!

Experiment 9

Coloring a Flower

You will need:
- scissors
- white flower with long stem such as a carnation
- red and blue food coloring
- two spoons
- two glasses
- water

Please ask an adult to help you trim the end of the flower stem. Then cut the stem along its length from the tip to just under the flower. This splits only the stem in half. Fill the two glasses with water. Add a few drops of red food coloring to one glass and a few drops of blue food coloring to the other. Mix the liquids well with the spoons.

Place one half of the stem into one glass and the other half of the stem in the other glass.

After a few
hours, look at the flower.
You should have a carnation that is half blue and
half red. The colored water in each glass moved
up the stem and into the flower. What other
color combinations can you make? Can
you make a flower with three colors?

To Find Out More

If you would like to learn more about plants, check out these additional resources.

Books

Durant, Penny Raife. **Exploring the World of Plants.** Franklin Watts, 1995.

George, Jean Craighead. **Acorn Pancakes, Dandelion Salad, and 38 Other Recipes.** Harper Collins Publishers, 1995.

Goldenberg, Janet. **Weird Things You Can Grow.** Random House, 1994.

Herd, Meg. **Learn and Play in the Garden.** Barron's Educational Series, 1997.

Talmage, Ellen. **Container Gardening for Kids.** Sterling Publishing Company, 1996.

Organizations and Online Sites

New England Wild Flower Society
180 Hemenway Road
Framingham, MA
01701-2699
508-877-7630
http://www.newfs.org/

You can find information about the oldest plant conservation organization in the United States. You can also order plants and seeds online.

The Herb Society of America
9019 Kirtland Chardon Road
Kirtland, OH 44094
440-256-0514
http://www.herbsociety. org/

You can get information about plants used as herbs. You can find out how to grow "A Child's Garden of Herbs" and look through a list of books that cover a wide variety of topics on plants.

International Carnivorous Plant Society
PMB 330
3310 East Yorba Linda Blvd.
Fullerton, CA 92831-1709
http://www. carnivorousplants.org/

Here you can learn about plants that eat animals.

Saskatchewan Education
2220 College Avenue
Regina, Saskatchewan
Canada
http://www.sasked.gov.sk. ca/docs/elemsci/g5fslc6. html

This site has a number of experiments on plants, including ones on how to grow plants without soil and how to measure the rate of root growth.

Important Words

chlorophyll chemical that makes plants green

embryo part of seed that grows into a new plant

evaporate to change into a vapor or gas

flower part of plant used to make a new plant

germinate to start to grow

osmosis how water moves into or out of a living thing, such as a plant

photosynthesis how plants make their own food

plant living thing that can make its own food

seed how most plants begin their lives

Index

Meet the Author

Salvatore Tocci is a science writer who lives in East Hampton, New York, with his wife, Patti. He was a high school biology and chemistry teacher for almost thirty years. As a teacher, he always encouraged his students to do experiments to learn about science. He and his wife have had little success in keeping deer from eating much of what they have planted. The only way they could protect their flowering plants was to put up a deer fence.

Photographs ©: Corbis-Bettmann: 7 bottom (Scott T. Smith), 22 (Ed Young); Dwight R. Kuhn Photography: 24, 30 (Dwight Kuhn); Envision: 21 (Brooks Walker); Innerspace Visions: 7 top (Mike Johnson); Photodisc: cover; Photo Researchers, NY: 10 (Geoff Bryant), 31 (E.R. Degginger), 36 top right (M.P. Kahl), 38 (Andrew Syred/SPL); Stone: 2 (Steve Taylor), 28 (Greg Vaughn); Visuals Unlimited: 1 (D. Cavagnaro), 4 (John Gerlach), 19 (Mark Newman), 36 top left (Kjell B. Sandved), 9 (John Sohlden).

Illustrations by Patricia Rasch